STEADFAST LOVE
Study Guide

Dr. Frank and Mary Alice Minirth
Dr. Brian and Dr. Deborah Newman
Dr. Robert and Susan Hemfelt

Compiled by Gary Wilde

THOMAS NELSON PUBLISHERS
NASHVILLE

Other Books in This Series

New Love Study Guide
Realistic Love Study Guide
Steadfast Love Study Guide
Renewing Love Study Guide
Transcendent Love Study Guide

The case examples presented in this book are fictional composites based on the authors' clinical experience with thousands of clients through the years. Any resemblance between these fictional characters and actual persons is coincidental. Two of the six authors, Mary Alice Minirth and Susan Hemfelt, are not psychotherapeutic clinicians and are not associated with the Minirth-Meier Clinic. The contributions of Mary Alice Minirth and Susan Hemfelt are derived from personal experience and their contribution makes no claim of professional expertise. Portions of this book that address clinical theory and clinical perspectives do not include contributions from Mary Alice Minirth and Susan Hemfelt.

Since many readers may read only one study guide in this series, we have repeated key concepts in more than one book. If you encounter this repetition, please be open to the possibility that these subjects are so vital, they bear such repetition.

The use of this study guide and the *Passages of Marriage* book is not intended as a substitute for professional counseling or psychotherapy. Serious individual or marital emotional problems should be referred to a competent psychiatric, psychological, or marriage and family therapy professional. The use of this study guide in a group study format under lay person leadership should be for educational purposes only. Groups that are psychotherapeutic in nature should always be facilitated by a licensed mental health professional.

Copyright © 1993 by Thomas Nelson Publishers

All rights reserved. Written permission must be secured from the publisher to use or reproduce any part of this book, except for brief quotations in critical reviews or articles.

Published in Nashville, Tennessee, by Thomas Nelson, Inc., and distributed in Canada by Lawson Falle, Ltd., Cambridge, Ontario.

Scripture quotations are from the NEW KING JAMES VERSION of the Bible. Copyright © 1979, 1980, 1982, Thomas Nelson, Inc., Publishers.

ISBN: 0-8407-4565-6

Printed in the United States of America

1 2 3 4 5 6 — 98 97 96 95 94 93

Contents

Introducing the *Passages* Study Guides   *v*

"My Spouse Is Like an Old Shoe . . . Can a Marriage Get Too Comfortable?"   *xi*

1. What Are the Passages of Marriage?   *1*
2. Can You Resist the Now-or-Never Syndrome?   *8*
3. Can You Truly Forgive?   *14*
4. Are You Prepared for the Inevitable Losses?   *19*
5. Is the Adolescent in Control, or Are You and Your Spouse?   *24*
6. Can Your Spouse Fulfill Your Need for Intimacy?   *30*

Leading the *Passages* Studies   *35*

Dr. Frank Minirth is a diplomate of the American Board of Psychiatry and Neurology. Along with Dr. Paul Meier, he founded the Minirth-Meier Clinic in Dallas, Texas, one of the largest psychiatric clinics in the United States.

Mary Alice Minirth is a homemaker and the mother of four children.

Dr. Brian Newman is the clinical director of inpatient services at the Minirth-Meier Clinic in Richardson, Texas. He received his M.A. in counseling from Grace Theological Seminary and his Doctorate of Philosophy from Oxford Graduate School.

Dr. Deborah Newman is a psychotherapist with the Minirth-Meier Clinic. She received her M.A. in counseling from Grace Theological Seminary and her Doctorate of Philosophy from Oxford Graduate School.

Dr. Robert Hemfelt is a psychologist with the Minirth-Meier Clinic who specializes in the treatment of chemical dependencies and compulsivity disorders.

Susan Hemfelt is a homemaker and the mother of three children.

For general information about other Minirth-Meier Clinic branch offices, counselling services, educational resources and hospital programs, call toll-free 1-800-545-1819. National Headquarters: (214) 669-1733 (800)229-3000.

Introducing the *Passages* Study Guides

You've made an excellent decision! You've decided to take some time out of your busy schedule in the next few weeks to focus on something that is very important to you, something that often gets taken for granted: your marriage. Your decision will launch you into an exploration of where you are in your marital journey and help you successfully navigate the next passages along your route to a more healthy, loving relationship with your spouse.

For Individual Study

As you work through the questions in this study guide, you will be reviewing and applying the principles taught in the Thomas Nelson book *Passages of Marriage,* by Frank and Mary Alice Minirth, Brian and Deborah Newman, and Robert and Susan Hemfelt. The Scripture readings and discussion questions will provide you with an excellent, nonthreatening entry into marriage enrichment. (If possible, get your spouse involved with you in this study.)

The five passages of a marriage are: 1) New Love, (which

we call Young Love in the original *Passages of Marriage*) the first two years; 2) Realistic Love, the third through the tenth years; 3) Steadfast Love, (called Comfortable Love in *Passages of Marriage*) the eleventh through the twenty-fifth years; 4) Renewing Love, the twenty-sixth through the thirty-fifth years; 5) Transcendant Love, the thirty-sixth year and on. This guide talks about the seven tasks of Steadfast Love. The first chapter considers two of those tasks and each chapter after that considers one of those tasks. By tasks we mean attitude changes one must make and jobs one must complete in order to maintain an intimate marital relationship.

The introductory paragraphs in each study are taken from *Passages of Marriage,* which is available in a hardcover edition and on video, and present the concept you will be considering. After jotting down your personal reactions to this concept, you'll study and apply a portion of Scripture related to the topic. Finally, you'll spend some time in prayer, praising God for insights gained and asking Him for greater strength to carry out what you've learned. Here, then, are the three main sections of the study guide which move you through this process:

1. *My Story:* The questions in this section emphasize your personal reflection. You'll recall the particular task of marriage you've considered: What insights, issues, or questions formed in your mind in response to the material? What past experiences do you remember that help you relate to the authors' examples? In what ways did your reading offer a new vision of your future role as a spouse?

2. *God's Story:* A natural progression in your Christian growth is first to consider, *Where am I?* then, *What is God calling me to do?* After that, you ask yourself, *Where do I need to move to live daily closer to His revealed will?* The coming together of My Story and God's Story creates some healthy inner tension. You'll benefit from this challenging form of self-discovery as it spurs you to make positive changes in attitude and actions.

The first three or four questions in this section relate directly to the Bible passage. They ask you to explore the content of God's Word and to consider its personal meaning for you and your marriage. You will be asking yourself things like: *What does this passage tell me about God's will for human relationships? How do these biblical principles relate to my relationship with my spouse? What do I find here that is intriguing, challenging, or convicting?*

The next set of questions helps you apply what you have learned from the Bible to one of the four tasks of Realistic Love. Here you'll be analyzing your marital relationship, based on the tasks required in your particular marriage passage.

3. *Prayer Moments:* As you read and study, you will no doubt realize that you have successfully completed some of the tasks in your marriage passage. This is cause for great joy. However, you will also recognize areas of your marriage that need strengthening. This study guide invites you to take some time to bring both your joys and ongoing concerns before the Lord in prayer. You may wish to use the suggested prayertime format or offer prayer in your own customary manner.

If You Are Studying with a Group

You may be using this guide along with a group of other couples who are in the same stage of marital development as you are. Your group may be led by a facilitator, or the group may choose to rotate leadership responsibilities weekly. Group study can be an excellent means of enriching your understanding of the passages; however, group educational study should never be confused with or substituted for group psychotherapy. Psychotherapeutic groups must always be facilitated by a licensed mental health professional. Each chapter of the guide covers a key element, or task, in your group's passage of marriage so everyone can be ready to join in group discussion. (See the Leading the *Passages* Studies section at the back of this guide, for detailed instructions on how to facilitate a group study of *Passages*.)

The key to enjoying a study series with others is to enter into discussion wholeheartedly. Be willing to share about yourself, your ideas, and your particular struggles at appropriate times. As you and others risk, truthfully revealing who you are, you will find yourselves growing closer together in a deepening bond of fellowship. Listening and responding to others' experiences will give you a more objective view of your own problems. You'll see that you are not alone in any of your struggles to maintain a healthy marriage; others have been where you are. People in your group will offer valuable insights, and you, in the same way, can aid others by sharing from your learned wisdom.

Most groups will have a good sense of how to relate to each other during the series of studies. However, it's probably best to make these assumptions explicit by putting them in an informal statement, or covenant, to which all can subscribe. Such a covenant could include:

- Regular attendance: *I commit to being here for each meeting unless an emergency situation calls me away. If I know I will miss a meeting, I will inform the leader in advance, if possible.*
- Promise of confidentiality: *I will hold in strict confidence the items of personal sharing revealed in these meetings.*
- Spirit of participation: *I will seek to become fully involved in conversation and sharing, as I feel led, and as I feel comfortable.*
- Direct, loving communication: *I will seek to maintain personal integrity by letting others know when I sense a problem in the way the group is relating to me.*
- Willingness to be available: *I will try to be available for others when they express a need for practical help or nurture. My phone number is* _____ .

- Referral to professional assistance: *If I recognize in myself or another group member the presence of serious individual or marital distress, I will seek or encourage that person to seek competent mental health care.*

Other Books in This Series

Each book in the *Passages* study guide series describes in detail one of the stages of marital development:

- New Love Study Guide
- Realistic Love Study Guide
- Renewing Love Study Guide
- Transcendent Love Study Guide

The books explain both the joys and potential hazards of each stage while giving clear, practical advice about how to navigate through those problem areas. Each of the marital stages demands the completion of specific tasks before a couple can move to the next stage. Where are you? What is your next task as a couple?

"My Spouse Is Like an Old Shoe . . . Can a Marriage Get Too Comfortable?"

The Third Passage of marriage requires couples to weave into the marital tapestry seven very different pieces of material: the tasks of Steadfast Love. The golden thread that runs through these tasks and makes them blend into the larger work—that gives them a common goal—is a deeper intimacy than the couple has ever known. Such intimacy cannot be spun from exaggerated dependence or exaggerated independence. Rather it is formed in a marital environment in which both partners work at helping each other achieve their God-given potentials in life and neither gets swallowed up in the other's dreams or goals.

One of the first tasks you will encounter in the *Steadfast Love Study Guide* is that of resisting the now-or-never syndrome. Couples encountering the threatening now-or-never syndrome are tempted to believe that getting out now will solve every problem that has arisen in their marriage. Now-or-never thinking wants to believe that an imperfect situation is better left alone than opened up to change and improvement. Steadfast Love, however, faces head-on the imperfections and sore spots of a relationship and gives them the attention they deserve. As couples attend to these imperfections, they must continue learning to offer one another ongoing forgiveness—the "seven times seventy" (Matt. 18:22) kind that Jesus proclaimed to Peter.

The art of forgiving, another of the tasks of Steadfast Love, needs to be practiced regularly. It is the secret of keeping a marriage alive. True forgiveness does not withhold love and acceptance until the other "goes first." Rather it shucks off bitterness and resentment and frees both partners to move forward.

A third task you will encounter is facing inevitable losses of life. You've no doubt come to the sudden revelation "I'm getting older by the minute!" Acknowledging and working through this is stressful. But every loss must surface and be grieved: the loss of youth, health, unfulfilled dreams and goals. As you complete this task and your old support systems crumble, you will learn to develop new goals and dreams.

We trust you will enjoy your creative venture, weaving your way through this Third Passage. And by the way, old shoes can be beautiful. They speak of myriad experiences: marching down a wedding aisle; carrying a sick child up hospital steps; walking through familiar halls of workplaces and grocery stores; moving among the graves of parents and friends. So many things have happened in your life and marriage so far! Don't discard them. Polish them in your memory. Cherish them in your heart. To be comfortable does not necessarily mean being bored. It can also mean experiencing a depth of calm and peace in being one.

Chapter 1

What Are the Passages of Marriage?

I*t's a solid hit into deep right field!"* the announcer screams exuberantly. *The ball is still airborne as the player rounds first. It drops into tall grass.... The player passes third, homeward bound.*

Wait! He failed to touch second! As his team groans in unison, he runs back to stomp second base. What would have been a home run ends up only a double, all because the runner failed to clear second base satisfactorily. Marriage is like that. We call the bases *"passages."*

First things first, right? You touch second before you race for third; you buckle up before you pull out of the driveway; you check your parachute before jumping out of the plane.

Passages of Marriage tells us that it's first things first in the married life, too. There are at least five distinct stages of development that every marriage must eventually navigate if it is to remain healthy and happy throughout its life. Each of these passages requires a couple to accomplish specific tasks before they can enter the next stage, regardless of the couple's age or the length of their marriage.

Of course, you need to know and understand what the

tasks are before you can work on completing them. You need to ask yourself: **How do these tasks relate to me and my unique marital journey?**

My Story

1. By choosing this study guide, you have determined that you are in the marital passage of Steadfast Love. What is your initial guess about the most pressing marital task(s) you need to accomplish at this point? Check one or more of these tasks (which you will be studying in the weeks ahead):

___ Task One: Maintain an Individual Identity Along with the Marriage Identity
___ Task Two: Say the Final Good-byes
___ Task Three: Overcome the Now-or-Never Syndrome
___ Task Four: Practice True Forgiveness
___ Task Five: Accept the Inevitable Losses
___ Task Six: Help Your Adolescent Become an Individual
___ Task Seven: Maintain an Intimate Relationship

2. To rebuild your personal identity, you could begin a "calendar of hope" (planning the next decade in terms of what you wish to do for yourself). What are some things you've dreamed of doing? Jot down some general planning notes about how and when you could begin to pursue one of these dreams. **(For instance, I've wanted to take a course in sculpture at the local community college; I've always wanted to try starting my own business.)**

3. If you were to write your parents a good-bye letter (even if they are deceased or unavailable), what points would you want to include? **(For instance, I'd want to recount the good memories; offer forgiveness for their failures.)**

God's Story

2 Peter 1:2–8
2 Grace and peace be multiplied to you in the knowledge of God and of Jesus our Lord,
3 as His divine power has given to us all things that pertain to life and godliness, through the knowledge of Him who called us by glory and virtue,
4 by which have been given to us exceedingly great and precious promises, that through these you may be partakers of the divine nature, having escaped the corruption that is in the world through lust.
5 But also for this very reason, giving all diligence, add to your faith virtue, to virtue knowledge,
6 to knowledge self-control, to self-control perseverance, to perseverance godliness,
7 to godliness brotherly kindness, and to brotherly kindness love.
8 For if these things are yours and abound, you will be neither barren nor unfruitful in the knowledge of our Lord Jesus Christ.

---

1. In this Scripture passage, Peter describes the Christian life as a developmental process. In the same way that our marriages must continue to develop, we grow spiritually as we add various personal traits to our lives: faith, virtue, knowledge, self-control, perseverance, godliness, kindness, love.

Pick one of these traits and imagine it being much more evident in your marital relationship. Tell how, specifically, this trait could help you overcome a problem in your marriage.

2. If you were to choose the key Christian trait(s) characterizing your marriage right now, which would you pick?

Which of the traits in the list would you, personally, like to display to a greater degree?

3. Through God's power we have been given "all things that pertain to life and godliness" (vs. 3). Name at least two areas of your marriage that could benefit from a new reliance on God's power or help. Describe how you would like to see God work in those areas.

4. "Our very nature throws into our marriage certain clinkers that we do not recognize and cannot anticipate." These clinkers (or time-release capsules from our past) can be turned from bad to good if we can find and manage the sources of trouble. List some of the time-release capsules that could "go off" in your marriage, related to the potential problem areas the authors suggest:

Chronic financial stress:

In-law problems and involvement:

Family imbalance and stress:

Emotional or psychological dysfunctions:

Other area(s):

Task One: Maintain an Individual Identity Along with the Marriage Identity

5. James and Lonna knew each other so well they could often know what the other was thinking without even asking. As couples live with one another over the years, they may become so welded together that their individuality suffers. In this case, each spouse's identity derives from the partner, not from the self.

What parts of your identity seem to spring from the "real you" inside?

What parts of your identity seem to be the result of an unhealthy over-identification with your spouse?

6 ■ Steadfast Love Study Guide

6. Codependency can take two main forms in a marriage. First, exaggerated dependence (enmeshment) of the two personalities can result in dull complacency. Second, with exaggerated independence, the marriage partners have almost nothing in common except irritation and friction. This situation can escalate into constant hostility, or it can become like a pendulum that swings between periods of hostility and extreme "lovey-dovey" closeness.

Does your marriage relationship at this point tend more toward Exaggerated Dependence or Exaggerated Independence? Describe a recent event or conversation to illustrate your response.

Task Two: Say the Final Good-byes

7. "Deep within each human heart lurks the yearning that somewhere, someone is waiting to step in and direct you in all the right moves. . . . The ancient childhood dream of perfect parents acting with godlike wisdom lingers on."

What past events/issues would you have to grieve and put behind you in order to say good-bye to this childhood dream?

8. "I can remember when it hit me," this friend recalls. "I was driving to the grocery store after reading the morning paper. All of a sudden the obvious struck me: None of our investments were safe. There was nowhere we could put our money and know without doubt it would be there for us. . . . There was no guarantee of anything for tomorrow. Whatever we had and whatever we did, we had it and did it by the grace of God."

A key part of Steadfast Love is coming to realize that no

human power can guarantee your security. Where do you, personally, find your ultimate security in life? Describe your level of satisfaction with your choice so far.

Prayer Moments

Lord, thank You for Your provision of the strength and help I need to fulfill my role in marriage. The most challenging task for me at this stage of my marriage is:

I ask Your help to:

Amen.

Chapter 2

Can You Resist the Now-or-Never Syndrome?

Ilona had thought of divorce. She felt it was either "now-or-never." After all she was thirty-three, and she wasn't sure she'd have much of a chance to remarry if she didn't do something now. Still the kids needed a family to be in, and what would she gain by a divorce? Reede would still be Reede, an irritating pain in the posterior, whether she was with him or not, and he was, after all, the children's father. . . .

The Third Passage of marriage confronts us with a dangerous, though extremely seductive, temptation: to believe that getting out *now* will solve everything.

The truth is, recognizing our disenchantments and dissatisfactions can have a positive result. These feelings of "now or never" can spur us into a renewed effort to make our marriages better. They can push us to build up our spouses rather than giving in to the same old critical attitudes.

But we have to decide what to do with the manifestly imperfect: leave it, or make it better. In light of the solid investment both parties have put into the relationship over the years, wouldn't it be a shame just to walk away?

Even those who are not struggling with the immediate desire to run can nevertheless relate to many of Ilona's feelings. Steadfast Love begins to feel like comfortable love. And "comfortable" can quickly lapse into "routine" or even boring. So here's a study for anyone who feels his or her marriage is starting to run on autopilot.

My Story

1. List some of the negative aspects of your mate's personality. List weaknesses, shortcomings, and things that irritate you. **(For instance, my husband always finds some excuse to be at work on Saturdays, avoiding prime family time.)**

2. "Frequently what seems to be a very disturbing factor to one spouse may actually be a mirror of some sort of unresolved pain in his or her family of origin. . . . But the spouse is overreacting to it." Might that be the case with any of the aspects you've listed above? How might one or more of them mirror problems in your childhood family? **(For instance, my father was a workaholic who regularly worked through the weekends.)**

3. List some of the positive things about your spouse, things you appreciate and are thankful for. **(For instance, my wife is a natural nurturer—with plants, pets, and me.)**

God's Story

Colossians 3:12–19

12 Therefore, as the elect of God, holy and beloved, put on tender mercies, kindness, humbleness of mind, meekness, longsuffering;

13 bearing with one another, and forgiving one another, if anyone has a complaint against another; even as Christ forgave you, so you also must do.

14 But above all these things put on love, which is the bond of perfection.

15 And let the peace of God rule in your hearts, to which also you were called in one body; and be thankful.

16 Let the word of Christ dwell in you richly in all wisdom, teaching and admonishing one another in psalms and hymns and spiritual songs, singing with grace in your hearts to the Lord.

17 And whatever you do in word or deed, do all in the name of the Lord Jesus, giving thanks to God the Father through Him.

18 Wives, submit to your own husbands, as is fitting in the Lord.

19 Husbands, love your wives and do not be bitter toward them.

---

1. What is the toughest part, for you, about "bearing with one another" (vs. 13) after a decade or more of marriage?

How has your personal acceptance of Christ's forgiveness affected your attitude toward your spouse?

2. Describe a time in your married life when the peace of God really did "rule" (vs. 15)—carried you through a tough time of conflict.

3. Paul gives two direct commands in verses 18 and 19. Rate the "obedience quotient" of you and your spouse on this scale:

1 _____ 5
Toeing the line   Out of control

Give examples to support your response:

4. The now-or-never syndrome is a response of fear: that things are getting worse, that they can't get better, that *if I don't get out now, I will never be able to build a better life.*
What is your biggest fear about your marriage relationship as you look forward to the next five years?

5. Our mate's weaknesses are often responsible for his or her strengths, as well. So both strengths and weaknesses together contribute to our mate's excellence. Specifically, how do you see this principle at work in your own mate?

6. Spouses must learn to "grieve through" and forgive the negative aspects of a spouse's actions and personality. What would this process mean for you? Be specific about the things you would need to do.

7. By the Third Passage the partners' sex life can become routine or even boring, usually predictable. Suppose you and your spouse were to plan a get-away weekend to rekindle the romance in your relationship. Describe a possible get-away scenario that you could discuss with your spouse:

8. "This is the passage when couples finally get around to making peace with the disparity between fantasy and reality, the dream and the day-to-day." In what ways have you made such peace?

What still needs peaceful resolution within you, or within your marriage?

9. According to the Minirth-Meier counselors, a negative comment offsets the good effects of three or four positive ones. Positive comments must outnumber negative comments by at least three to one.
Think through your past ten days with your spouse. What's the ratio of positive comments (compliments or affirmations) to negative comments (put-downs or criticisms)? Jot down a specific example of each kind of comment that has been spoken.

Try one issue free...

That's right! We're so convinced that you will love **TODAY'S BETTER LIFE**, the full-color quarterly magazine from the experts at the Minirth-Meier Clinics, that we will send you an issue *absolutely free* when you return this card.

In it you'll find practical advice on improving your health, strengthening relationships, and growing in your faith. And all of the articles are written by experts committed to helping you grow stronger emotionally, physically, and spiritually.

Return this card or call our toll free number to start down the path to better life *today*.

☐ **YES,** I want to take advantage of this special offer for **TODAY'S BETTER LIFE.** Send me my free issue. If I like what I see, I'll pay only $16.95 for a one-year subscription. If not, I'll write "cancel" on the invoice and owe nothing.

NAME: _____

ADDRESS: _____

CITY: _____ STATE: _____ ZIP: _____

Or call toll free: 1-800-982-0500

■ BALANCE YOUR LIFE
■ DEEPEN YOUR FAITH
■ IMPROVE YOUR HEALTH

Please allow 4-6 weeks for your first issue to arrive. Offer good in U.S. only. Standard rate is $19.80 for four issues.

EBW02-2

BUSINESS REPLY MAIL
FIRST CLASS MAIL PERMIT NO. 619, MARION, OH

POSTAGE WILL BE PAID BY ADDRESSEE

TODAY'S BETTERLIFE

P.O. Box 1924

Marion, OH 43306-2024

NO POSTAGE
NECESSARY
IF MAILED
IN THE
UNITED STATES

10. "Finally, Ilona determined to settle in for the long haul. This would be no instant zap cure, no course of antibiotics and *presto!* the infection's gone. It would take time—the rest of the marriage, quite probably. She prepared herself for that."

If you see this as a wise decision, list three or four reasons why:

Why would "settling in" be a wise or foolish decision in your own case?

Prayer Moments

Lord, I give thanks for these positive things I see in the person You gave me to love:

Help me to be more aware of my own shortcomings in this relationship, particularly:

Amen.

Chapter 3

Can You Truly Forgive?

In some families, after blowups, everyone drifts off. Then they return slowly into good graces again until the next blowup. "I'm talking to you again" means "I forgive you." But the forgiveness isn't actually done or spoken. Putting it behind is not forgiving, per se. Calming down is not dealing with it. We must be willing to go back, address, and resolve the issues, or they'll just keep reappearing.

We're not talking here about nice, neat feelings. When a spouse commits adultery, for instance, you don't just smile and say: "That's okay; no problem." It hurts so bad, it takes your breath away. You feel rage like you never felt before; you want to scream, hit, kick. You're mad at your spouse and you boil with hatred for the third party, who so arrogantly forced entry into what was private territory.

Forgiveness. In a seething cauldron of hurt, hatred, and vows of revenge, is it possible?

My Story

1. How was anger handled in your family of origin? Describe a specific scenario that illustrates your response. (**For instance, in my family, anger was never considered appropriate; it was considered a "negative" emotion.**)

2. How was forgiveness practiced and carried out in your family of origin? Describe a specific scenario that illustrates your response. (**For instance, as a child I could be forgiven, but I always had to pay the price of being reminded occasionally of how bad I had been.**)

3. How do you and your spouse handle anger and forgiveness in your marriage? Describe a specific scenario that illustrates your response. (**For instance, we mostly avoid dealing with our anger directly; we get back at each other in subtle ways.**)

God's Story

Matthew 18:21–35
21 Then Peter came to Him and said, "Lord, how often shall my brother sin against me, and I forgive him? Up to seven times?"
22 Jesus said to him, "I do not say to you, up to seven times, but up to seventy times seven.
23 "Therefore the kingdom of heaven is like a certain king who wanted to settle accounts with his servants.

24 "And when he had begun to settle accounts, one was brought to him who owed him ten thousand talents.
25 "But as he was not able to pay, his master commanded that he be sold, with his wife and children and all that he had, and that payment be made.
26 "The servant therefore fell down before him, saying, 'Master, have patience with me, and I will pay you all.'
27 "Then the master of that servant was moved with compassion, released him, and forgave him the debt.
28 "But that servant went out and found one of his fellow servants who owed him a hundred denarii; and he laid hands on him and took him by the throat, saying, 'Pay me what you owe!'
29 "So his fellow servant fell down at his feet and begged him, saying, 'Have patience with me, and I will pay you all.'
30 "And he would not, but went and threw him into prison till he should pay the debt.
31 "So when his fellow servants saw what had been done, they were very grieved, and came and told their master all that had been done.
32 "Then his master, after he had called him, said to him, 'You wicked servant! I forgave you all that debt because you begged me.
33 " 'Should you not also have had compassion on your fellow servant, just as I had pity on you?'
34 "And his master was angry, and delivered him to the torturers until he should pay all that was due to him.
35 "So My heavenly Father also will do to you if each of you, from his heart, does not forgive his brother his trespasses."

---

1. What do you believe was Peter's motive in asking his question about the "appropriate" amount of forgiveness to extend to a repeating offender?

2. What is your personal reaction to Jesus' response in verse 22?

How would you apply this response, practically, to a conflict situation or a hurt you face in your marriage right now?

3. Parables make one key point. In which verse is the point driven home in this parable? Put this key point into your own words, with reference to your marital relationship:

4. What does it mean for you to forgive "from your heart" (vs. 35)?

5. When two married people get embroiled in angry conflict they will usually find hurt—or the fear of hurt—at the bottom of the situation.
Recall a recent argument with your spouse. List some of the hurts and fears inside you that helped fuel the conflict.

6. Some people believe in "instantaneous" forgiveness—that there should be no lingering hurt or anger. But forgiveness is *not* forgetting; it does not erase memories, remove the hurt, or eliminate the need to keep working on a relationship. What hurts are you still grieving, even after forgiving?

7. Forgiveness is a command, a decision we make, regardless of our feelings. How would it benefit you and your mate to approach forgiveness this way?

8. When we are hurt, we want to lash back. But to forgive our spouses, we must yield our rights to retribution. How hard is it for you to give up this right?

9. Some people think forgiving an act like adultery means approving of an unforgivable act. How would you explain to such a person where his thinking had gone wrong?

10. "Most medical practitioners agree that in our modern society, up to 50 percent of physical disorders are significantly, if not primarily, stress related."
Where does stress tend to "reside" in your body?

How much of your stress would you say is internally generated (related to old anger, bitterness, resentment)?

Prayer Moments

Heavenly Father, thank You for providing healing for my deep hurts. I want to initiate a conversation with my spouse about:

I ask Your help to relinquish my bitterness in the area of:

Amen.

Chapter 4

Are You Prepared for the Inevitable Losses?

"When I graduated from high school I was going to change the world. By the time I finished college I hoped to make my mark in America. In graduate school, I thought I might change a little of Arkansas. Now I'd be content to redecorate my office."

Where did all those dreams go? And so fast!

Suddenly, you're looking back as much as you're looking ahead. In fact, it's almost easier now to dwell on the things that might have been rather than the things that still can be. *If only* . . . .

This chapter can help you recognize what's happening. Things have changed. Some of the old support systems have crumbled. You're searching for replacements. Old responsibilities have drifted into the wind (your kids leave home). New roles come crashing in (your parents need help).

The Third Passage confronts you with your losses while challenging you to latch on to the new goals and dreams that will pull you through the years ahead. Like Tarzan, swinging from one grapevine to the next, may you learn to let go and learn to go on.

My Story

1. Think: When did it actually hit you that you "aren't getting any younger"? What impact has the inevitability of aging had on you recently?

2. Meditate on some of the losses you've suffered to this point in your life. What would you name as the most painful ones—those that need to be grieved in the days ahead?

3. What were your vocational dreams at age 20? age 30? To what extent have they been fulfilled?

God's Story

2 Corinthians 4:8–9, 16–18
8 We are hard pressed on every side, yet not crushed; we are perplexed, but not in despair;
9 persecuted, but not forsaken; struck down, but not destroyed—. . . .
16 Therefore we do not lose heart. Even though our outward man is perishing, yet the inward man is being renewed day by day.
17 For our light affliction, which is but for a moment, is working for us a far more exceeding and eternal weight of glory,

18 while we do not look at the things which are seen, but at the things which are not seen. For the things which are seen are temporary, but the things which are not seen are eternal.

---

1. What do the four "yets/buts" in verses 8 and 9 tell you about the apostle Paul's attitude toward crisis and hardship?

2. In what specific ways is it possible for the "outward man" to perish while the "inward man" gets renewed? Describe your own experience with this phenomenon.

3. Have you ever felt that you "lost heart" in the face of a challenge or crisis in your marriage (vs. 16)?

What part did/could spiritual renewal play in this situation?

4. Do you agree that contrasting present "light afflictions" with a future "eternal weight of glory" (vs. 17) is a good way to encourage a Christian believer? Why or why not?

5. Overall, would you say your eyes are more focused on the "here and now" or the "yet to come"?

What might be the benefit to you—and to your marriage—if you paid more attention to the "things which are not seen" (vs. 18)?

6. Mid-life brings a drastic change in one's support base, due to the many losses that occur (especially the loss of parents as guides and protectors). What would you name as your top three sources of personal support during crisis and change?

How satisfied are you with your present support system?

7. "This is now the time of either crisis or growth, a major Y in the tree of decisions. Crises will either destroy you or generate new intimacy and growth."
As you look over your past responses to crisis and change, would you say that most often you have tended to grow or tended to move closer to "destruction"? Give an example to support your response.

8. As a marriage grows and becomes stronger, through mid-life the partners gain a greater ability to "roll with the punches."
Recall a marital crisis you went through in the first two years and tell how you would handle such a crisis now.

In light of your response, what evidence do you see of growth in wisdom and in coping ability in your mid-life?

9. The Minirth-Meier doctors encourage everyone in mid-life to stay on top of potential health problems. What can you do to prevent potential health problems?

Prayer Moments

Lord, I am grateful for the things You have allowed me to accomplish so far. My most painful unfulfilled dream is:

Please help me adjust to my losses and move ahead in this area:

Amen.

Chapter 5

Is the Adolescent in Control, or Are You and Your Spouse?

As a tactical maneuver, the adolescent may try to provoke the parent into taking a stand. The child wants a solid wall; instead he's feeling a padded cell. The potential for dangerous escalation then is unlimited. The more the teenager acts out to express all those needs and frustrations and anger, deliberately causing friction and getting into trouble, the more uncertain the parent becomes about his or her own abilities—the wall becomes still less solid, the teen bounces off it still more wildly, trying to find a firm surface. And down and down it spirals, to disaster.

The times have changed. The styles are different. The diversions and temptations come with more options, perhaps. But being a teen is still the same uphill struggle that it was a few decades ago. So put yourself back in the shoes of the budding adolescent. Once again face those conflicting twin messages hurtling at you from the adult world: *Stop acting so childish. . . . You're not a grown-up, you know.* How do you feel?

We value independent thinking and aggressiveness in adults, right? So how will teens develop such traits if they can't try them out on their parents? Teenage rebellion has just got to happen. Get ready for the stress and strain on your marriage.

As your adolescent struggles to bridge the gap between childlike needs and adult responsibility, he or she may feel caught in a quagmire of conflicting expectations and confusing rules. This chapter calls parents to offer firm support and clear guidance. By shoring up their own marriage, a parenting team can help turn the marshy fields of adolescence into a highway leading to wise young adulthood for their children.

My Story

1. How safe was it for you, as a teen, to come to your parents with *any* personal problem, concern, or feeling? (**For instance, I was given the clear signal that "not rocking the boat" was the best way to get approval.**)

2. Consider the male and female role models you grew up with. What positive and negative attitudes did they pass on to you about what it means to be a man or a woman? (**For instance, I'm thankful that my father was able to model masculine gentleness for me.**)

3. The Minirth-Meier counselors say that teens want to know—in solid black and white terms—where the behavioral boundaries are. How clear were the "rules" in your family of

origin when you were a teen? **(For instance, the rules were confusing and changed a lot, keeping me guessing about what was appropriate.)**

God's Story

Luke 2:40-50
40 And the Child grew and became strong in spirit, filled with wisdom; and the grace of God was upon Him.
41 His parents went to Jerusalem every year at the Feast of the Passover.
42 And when He was twelve years old, they went up to Jerusalem according to the custom of the feast.
43 When they had finished the days, as they returned, the Boy Jesus lingered behind in Jerusalem. And Joseph and His mother did not know it;
44 but supposing Him to have been in the company, they went a day's journey, and sought Him among their relatives and acquaintances.
45 So when they did not find Him, they returned to Jerusalem, seeking Him.
46 Now so it was that after three days they found Him in the temple, sitting in the midst of the teachers, both listening to them and asking them questions.
47 And all who heard Him were astonished at His understanding and answers.
48 So when they saw Him, they were amazed; and His mother said to Him, "Son, why have You done this to us? Look, Your father and I have sought You anxiously."
49 And He said to them, "Why is it that you sought Me? Did you not know that I must be about My Father's business?"

50 But they did not understand the statement which He spoke to them.

---

1. Verse 40 presents a very attractive picture of adolescent growth—becoming strong, wise, spiritually blessed. How does this picture compare with your own dreams for your child's development in the coming years? Be specific.

2. In verse 43, we are told that Jesus "lingered behind" His parents. How might this be considered an aspect of the process of individuation?

3. Put yourself in the place of Mary and Joseph (in vss. 44–48), who were quite annoyed with the actions of their son. How upset would you be in a similar circumstance? Put your words of reprimand (see vs. 48) in your own typical words to your teen.

4. In light of verses 49 and 50, what deeper understandings about their son's inner life would have helped Mary and Joseph do a better job of parenting?

What attempts have you made recently to know your teen's inner life—his or her true feelings?

5. In trying to attain individuation, a teen "must shift his whole being from family member to solo individual, from governed to capable-of-self-government, from child-treated-like-a-child to adult-peer-of-adults."
How easy or difficult is it for you to accept your teen's emerging adulthood?

6. Teenager James was living out the rebellion against his father that James's mother never expressed against *her* father. In this way, the mother's control issue got passed on to the son.
What control issue from your past do you feel you must guard against "bequeathing" to your own children in this way?

7. "It's emotionally vary scary if one parent lays down a rule and the other undercuts, invalidates, or excuses that rule."
What happened the last time you or your mate undercut each other in dealing with your teen's behavior?

8. Teens need lots of affirmation during this period characterized by self-doubt. Jot down the latest words of encouragement or praise you gave your teen:

If you can't remember a recent affirmation, what would you like to say to him or her at the next appropriate time?

9. Many parents have overly invested their own self-esteem in their kids. Yet parents' self-images should not depend on a child being smart or accomplished.

Where has the line been blurred a bit between your own self-esteem and your child's "performance"?

10. How willing are you to give your teen the most precious freedom of all—the freedom to make mistakes and fail?

Prayer Moments

Lord, one thing that really concerns me about my ability to be a good parent is:

Please give me the courage to set a better example by:

Amen.

Chapter 6

Can Your Spouse Fulfill Your Need for Intimacy?

"If we had an evening together, it meant the secretaries made a scheduling error," said Jane Fonda, commenting on her divorce from Tom Hayden. Two busy lives flung in different orbits can wreck intimacy. Your life doesn't have to be as busy as a movie star's either. The common pressures and distractions of modern life suffice.

How is it with you? Do you feel really close to your mate? If not, read on. There are definite warning signs, symptoms, and solutions to the problem of waning intimacy in the Third Passage.

As usual, the solutions get you involved in processes of mutual sharing and healing. This takes time and effort but culminates in a new appreciation for the intriguing mind, body, and soul you've been given the privilege of exploring for the rest of your life—your spouse.

My Story

1. Are there any old family of origin wounds that seem to keep you from fully revealing yourself to your mate? List some possibilities. **(For instance, my mother once scolded me for "sounding like a cow" when I cried; I've been afraid to cry in front of my wife.)**

2. What wounds have been inflicted in your own marriage that might have caused you to pull back from a deepening intimacy? **(For instance, I find it hard to forget about his cheating on me ten years ago.)**

3. What assumptions are you making about how your spouse sees you? List some ways these assumptions could possibly be distorted. **(For instance, I always thought my spouse saw me as too aggressive in lovemaking—until I asked him/her about it.)**

God's Story

Job 13:20–24
20 "Only two things do not do to me,
Then I will not hide myself from You:

21 Withdraw Your hand far from me,
And let not the dread of You make me afraid.

22 Then call, and I will answer;
Or let me speak, then You respond to me.

23 How many are my iniquities and sins?
Make me know my transgression and my sin.

24 Why do You hide Your face,
And regard me as Your enemy?"

---

1. Have you ever felt the desire to hide from God because of fear of rejection? (see vs. 20) Describe your experience.

2. How do the two things Job asked of God mirror two big fears we often have in our marital relationships?

3. Job, in his desperate situation, invited God to look deep within his soul to find transgression and sin. How willing are you to be "evaluated" by God, as Job asked? (see vs. 23) By your spouse, in a session of candid discussion about mutual shortcomings? Do you feel you have to wait until you have reached the point of desperation?

4. "When love dies, it's not in the heat of battle. It's when a partner believes the other will never meet the needs for intimacy."
To what extent are your needs for intimacy being met right now? How much hope do you have for a greater fulfillment of your needs in the future?

5. Jean said she thought she had a near perfect marriage. "Anger? Oh no. . . . We never hurt each other." What suspicions are raised in your mind when you hear such a statement?

6. Constantly giving unsolicited advice to a partner can be a way of avoiding good listening and comfort-giving. What unsolicited advice has been given or received between you and your spouse lately? What real needs (yours and your spouse's) would you guess underlie those advice-giving sessions?

7. One of the feelings that can help intimacy quietly slip away is: "I no longer trust you to prioritize me." Put a mark on the line to show where your trust level is in this regard.

■ _____ ■
I'm tops on   I'm way down,
his/her list   almost outta sight

Mark where you think your spouse would respond. What topic for discussion could this exercise raise for you?

8. Below are specific warning signs that repairs to intimacy are called for. Choose one and describe the problem. Then jot down some notes about a potential approach to dealing with the problem.

___ sexual difficulties
___ power struggles
___ financial struggles

___ excessive or malicious fighting
___ physical separation

9. Rick and Nancy sat down for a round of businesslike negotiating. "If you do such and so, I'll do so and so." As cold and mechanistic as it was, it got the attitude of sharing back in place again.

What are you willing to give in order to get at this point in your marriage? List some items here:

I COULD GIVE	I NEED TO GET
•	•
•	•
•	•
•	•
•	•

Prayer Moments

Lord, I'm so afraid to reveal my true self in the area of:

Give me the courage and wisdom to approach my spouse soon, in a nonthreatening way, about this specific need:

Amen.

Leading the *Passages* Studies

Do you enjoy getting to know people through significant conversation? Do you want to strengthen your marriage through study and discussion with your spouse and with other couples? Would you like to share with others the things you've learned from experience and the Scriptures—things that can help them, too? Leading a group through *Passages of Marriage* is a wonderful opportunity for you to do all of these things as you help others learn and grow.

Getting Started

You can use this study guide in a variety of settings and time frames. For instance, your group could meet either weekly, bi-weekly, or monthly; it could meet in a home, during a Sunday School or mid-week hour at church. An informal home setting, with minimal time constraints, is probably best, however, since it will encourage a greater depth of sharing.

Consider having a low-key introductory meeting before launching into the sessions in this study guide. At this meeting, you would distribute the study guides and give participants a chance to meet and get acquainted with each other. You could then offer a brief explanation of *Passages of Marriage* and talk about how you plan to proceed with the series. Get group members' comments and suggestions about how to schedule and structure your times together. Participants could then be asked to share some of their expectations for the sessions.

You may also wish to ask couples to tell their stories in this initial session. Give couples as much time as they want, even if you have to schedule some of the stories on different nights. Couples should share significant details about: their early lives as individuals, their families of origin, how they met, and what they see as the cutting-edge issue in their marriages right now. Be sure each partner has a chance to talk. Ask specific questions of one of the partners, if necessary.

Ideally, you will have two to six couples in your group. Everyone should have a copy of both the *Passages* book and this study guide. Participants may read the appropriate pages from *Passages* during the week, or they may do the reading and fill in their guides together during the study time—it's up to you and your group to decide what will work best in light of people's home and work schedules. (Note: You may wish to invite some single participants, too; those who are contemplating marriage or those who wish to review the history of a failed marriage in hopes of gaining skills for the future.)

Begin each session by reading the introductory paragraphs aloud to refresh group members' memories about the topic under study. If you have time, ask for personal reactions to the introduction. Then ask a volunteer to read the Bible passage aloud. (If you get no volunteers, read the passage yourself. Don't call on people; you'll risk embarrassing someone who is uncomfortable reading in public.) Proceed through each of the three main sections of the guide, drawing on the supplemental material found in the Leader's Notes for each study.

Use the discussion method of leading the group through the My Story and God's Story sections. Remember that adults thrive on discussion for a number of reasons: 1) it calls upon them to use and develop their analysis skills; 2) it lets them contribute from the storehouse of wisdom they've gained through years of experience; 3) it allows them to clarify and process what they've learned; 4) it offers the opportunity to develop interpersonal skills that can enhance their marital communication.

The Prayer Moments section offers individuals the opportunity to jot down their concerns and bring their desires before the Lord, privately. Use your knowledge of your group's unique personality to decide how, or whether to use this section for group sharing and discussion. Some volunteers may wish to share what they have written; some groups may feel comfortable doing this every week. Other groups will simply structure a more general group prayer time that is comfortable for them.

Preparing for Group Leadership

As you prepare to lead, consider these five pieces of general advice that can promote any leader's success with a group:

Study through all six of the sessions yourself, in advance, to get a good grasp of the Bible passages and a feel for the questions you'll want to emphasize in discussion. As you study, jot down points of particular interest or any ideas you have about how to deal with certain issues in a group setting. Formulate your own responses to the questions and recall events or stories from your own experience that you could share with the group at appropriate points.

Plan on including key ingredients for building a solid group life in your sessions. Structure some time for sharing and prayer. Perhaps offer light refreshments around which people can get to know each other socially before or after the study time.

Decide how you will handle absenteeism. As leader, one of your responsibilities will be to follow up on those who miss sessions, letting them know they are missed. Find out if they foresee any problems getting to the next meeting. Ask if you can help them solve any problems with transportation, childcare, etc.

Help your group members develop feelings of closeness as your study series unfolds. As the group members loosen up over the weeks, they'll begin feeling freer to share their real lives and struggles in meaningful ways. Be sure you include many of the sharing and application-type questions in every study. Don't limit your group to simply discussing what the author said without asking them to tell how they feel about it.

Avoid group burnout. A group can get burned out when it never varies in intensity and seems to require a lifetime commitment. To counteract this potential problem, request short-term commitments for studies of deep intensity (like this six session plan) and longer-term commitment for studies that involve less intensity. Be prepared to take chunks of time off between study series to give people a chance to assimilate what they've learned.

Using a Facilitator Approach

Act as a growth facilitator rather than as a teacher in leading these studies. A facilitating group leader: provides a structure for igniting discussion and building friendships; stimulates participation through wise use of discussion questions; encourages and affirms others' attempts to learn and discuss; models personal transparency by sharing about personal struggles as well as strengths. So, as a facilitator, you will find yourself summarizing group discussions and feelings, describing reactions of the group to ideas or issues, and helping the group go through conflict in productive ways. You can do all this if you simply have a desire to serve, a willingness to learn, and a commitment to spending significant time in preparation.

Note that the facilitator approach means a group leader is NOT:

- a person who always has the answer;
- a person who does most of the talking in the group;
- a person who takes total responsibility for everyone enjoying themselves;
- a person who perfectly displays, in his or her marriage, the principles being studied;
- a person who competes with others to produce the best ideas, or ask the most brilliant questions.
- a person who attempts to be a marriage therapist to other couples.

Working with Couples in a Group

You are not expected to be a marriage counselor during these sessions! However, knowing some basic principles of interpersonal relating can help you work with your couples:

Let couples be themselves. There are many ways to live out a happy marriage, and each marital contract has its uniqueness. Accept people where they are and simply offer these studies as a means for exploring possible relational improvements in ways *the couples themselves* may decide upon.

Learn to accept emotions expressed in the group. This particular study is quite different from the typical Bible study. Because couples will discuss aspects of their marriages, emotions will no doubt come into play. Let everyone know from the outset that emotions are normal and natural, though sometimes uncomfortable. If someone cries, offer Kleenex but do *not* ask the person to stop. Accept the tears, let them do their cleansing work, spend some time in silence, and move on in the discussion. Group members around the crying individual may offer appropriate comfort.

Respond to possible conflict situations with helpful techniques. If individuals feel anger, it is entirely appropriate for them to own that anger and to state the reasons for it. However, ask group members to: 1) Use "I" statements when airing a complaint to a spouse ("I feel angry when this happens" rather than, "You make me angry when . . ."). An "I" statement shares about one's inner responses rather than being an attack on someone else. 2) Use the "and" method when offering a criticism. Often couples will say: "You do a great job at _____, BUT you don't . . ." The second half of the statement tends to wipe out the first half. It's better if the *but* can be replaced with *and*. Then both statements can stand together with equal power. 3) Share how they *feel*. Help couples discuss crucial issues on more than just the intellectual level. They *do* need to understand certain things. But truth must have impact on the whole person if it is to lead to personal growth.

Help group members apply important principles by occasionally asking, in a generic way, "How could someone put this idea into practice?" You are taking some pressure off by making the application general and helping participants envision it's workable.

Learn to use a debriefing process at points in your discussion. When couples share about a specific event or experience, help them go into more detail for the benefit of themselves and the group. When appropriate, gently draw them out: 1) What happened? 2) Who was involved? 3) How did you feel at the time, and after the event? 4) Why do you think things turned out as they did? 5) Were you surprised by anything that transpired? Why? 6) What do you *wish* would have happened instead? What could you have done differently? 7) What things did you learn from this experience about yourself, your spouse, or your marriage?

Handling Potential Problems

If nobody talks. In general, don't be afraid of silence, even long stretches of it. Adults need a certain amount of space as they think about how to respond to a discussion question. Usually, the silence is this productive, thinking kind. But if you sense that the silence indicates confusion or lack of interest, either rephrase your question or move on to the next one.

If someone dominates discussion. Occasionally you will have an over-talker in a group. Try some indirect solutions to this problem first: avoid eye contact after asking a question, or say something like, "Let's hear from others who have been a bit more quiet so far." Or: "How do the rest of you respond to Jack's comment?" If indirect methods fail to solve the problem, try a more direct approach. After the study you may need to pull this person aside and say: "I've noticed how enthused you are about participating in the discussion. Great! But I'm concerned about giving everyone a chance to speak . . ."

If discussion drifts and loses focus. Gently point out that the discussion has moved off track. However, ask the group if this really is something they want to pursue. Perhaps the issue is important enough to merit significant discussion.

If people are unfamiliar with the Bible. Some or all of the participants may have very little Bible background. Fine; here is a chance for them to learn! Let the group know from the beginning that no comment or question will be considered stupid or inappropriate. Consistently demonstrate that no one needs to be embarrassed by a lack of knowledge or by feeling misinformed. And do acknowledge each contribution. If someone directly espouses a serious doctrinal error, simply say: "Thank you for your contribution, Sally, but were you aware that most Christians have understood it this way . . . ?"

If members of the group begin to display high levels of emotional discomfort or marital stress, they should be urged to seek immediate medical, psychological, or pastoral care. This study group is not psychotherapy and should never be offered as a substitute for professional psychological or medical care. Your minister or pastoral care person should be able to assist you in locating competent referral resources.

Evaluating Your Group Experience

You will become a better group leader over the years if you take time to evaluate each of your group-leading experiences. This can be done after a series of group sessions (like these six), or at any time during the duration of the study series. Use questions like these as a personal checklist of your growth in group leadership skills:

___ Did I see any indications of personal and spiritual growth among the members of the group? Describe specific details.

___ Did I enjoy my role as a group facilitator?

___ Was I consistently sensitive to the needs of individuals in the group?

___ Was I able to exercise sufficient flexibility in my plans for each meeting, in order to meet the needs of the group?

___ What do I recall as my strengths?

___ What were my weaknesses? How do I know? What can I do to improve next time?

___ To what extent was I prepared or unprepared each week? What can I do to improve my preparedness in future group leadership?

___ What feedback did I get from participants during the course of the study series? What specific comments do I remember?

___ Do I feel personally affirmed in my role of group leadership? Why?

___ Am I growing in love for people and commitment to

the group process as a means of discipling others? How do I know?

Study 1. What Are the Passages of Marriage?
2 Peter 1:2–8

Aim: To introduce the concept of marriage passages and the first two tasks of Steadfast Love.

[Note: This study guide session covers material in *Steadfast Love*, chapters one and two.]

Question 1. Peter understood that new believers in Christ may begin with an enthusiasm that could wear off if they were not diligent in continuing to develop their spiritual lives. Moral progress was essential. As one wise Christian put it, "The Christian life must not be an initial spasm followed by a chronic inertia."

Help your group members see the parallels between Christian growth and the growth of their marital relationships. Those relationships, too, must be nurtured and "added to" with knowledge, self-control, patience, etc. The initial wonder, or infatuation, of Young Love does wear off. But a deeper love can begin to shine through.

Question 3. If God has given us "all things that pertain to life" then we can assume we have the resources and strength from Him to fulfill our marital roles in the most excellent way. However, this does *not* mean that our spouses will also rely on those same resources. This can cause us pain when we realize that we can only contribute our own best and hope that our spouses will respond in kind. Sometimes that does not happen. Encourage your group members to talk about how they, personally, find strength in God's help and promises without resorting to trying to change their spouses.

Question 4. Invite volunteers to share specific "clinkers" that they have either experienced or anticipate in the future. You may wish to have couples discuss together in private some possible "solutions" to the problem areas they identified.

Question 6. Stress that the goal is healthy interdependence. In this situation, neither spouse is unduly responsible for everything in the marriage—having all the feelings, taking care of all the chores.

Point out, too, that a certain amount of dependence is good. We all need to depend on one another. Sometimes, the burden of helping or nurturing naturally shifts back and forth between the spouses as one or the other goes through tough times.

Question 7. Ask volunteers to be specific about how they may still feel this yearning for parental guidance and protection. Mention that we never really grow out of our desire for approval from our parents, either. No matter how old we are, we are still their children. Yet, we can make some landmark decisions to untie any "apron strings" that adversely affect our adult decision-making processes or hinder our ability to relate to our spouses.

Question 8. Discussion of this question offers the opportunity to point to Jesus Christ as the one who offers ultimate security. Be prepared to share the basics of the Gospel message, should the situation seem appropriate. Do this in terms of *sharing your own experience*; avoid preachiness.

Study 2. Can You Resist the Now-or-Never Syndrome? Colossians 3:12–19

Aim: To consider the role of long-suffering and forgiveness in counteracting the temptation to run from a marital relationship.

Question 1. Ask volunteers to tell about their attempts to bear with one another. To shed light on the word meanings here, you may wish to share this quote from *The Expositor's Bible Commentary*, vol. 11 (Zondervan, p. 215): "Two Greek participles (*anechomenoi*, "bear with" and *charizomenoi*, "forgive") expand the thought of patience. Paul uses them to show that Christians who are truly patient will manifest this attitude by (1) a willingness to bear with those whose faults or unpleasant traits are an irritant to them and (2) a willingness to forgive those they have grievances against. 'Bear with' suggests the thought of putting up with things we dislike in others."

Question 2. The Greek word for "rule" in verse 15 originally had the meaning of "acting as an umpire" in an athletic arena. God's peace can be allowed to make the final decision in disputes. We can commit to avoiding actions and attitudes that would hinder the flow of this peace in our marriages.

Question 3. Verses 18 and 19 can be considered a specific application of the general principle set down in verse 17. Point out that, in general, Paul's call for mutual responsibility in marriage went against the prevailing culture in which a wife was considered little more than a possession. William Barclay (in *The Daily Study Bible, Philippians, Colossians, and Thessalonians*, p. 161) commented: "Under Jewish law a woman was a thing, the possession of her husband, just as much as his house or his flocks or his material goods. She had no legal rights whatever. For instance, under Jewish law, a husband could divorce his wife for any cause, while a wife had no rights whatever in the initiation of divorce; and the only grounds on which divorce might be awarded her were if her husband developed leprosy, became an apostate or ravished a virgin.

"In Greek society a respectable woman lived a life of entire seclusion. She never appeared on the streets alone, not even to go marketing. She lived in the women's apartments and did not join her menfolk even for meals. From her there was demanded complete servitude and chastity; but her husband could go out as much as he chose and could enter into as many relationships outside marriage as he liked without incurring any stigma."

Question 5. Often a "weakness" is manifested as a "strength" when it is applied in the right context, and in the right proportions. So it is possible to help our spouses' weaknesses to be transformed into positive attributes.

Question 8. Mention that "making peace" is not the same as giving up on the marriage. Rather, making peace means taking a realistic approach to both: the dreams that were unrealistic; the new goals that a couple can develop for the future.

Study 3. Can You Truly Forgive?
Matthew 18:21-35

Aim: To recognize the need for true forgiveness in a marriage and to identify the steps it requires.

Question 1. In Jewish rabbinic thought, a brother was to be forgiven a repeated sin three times. The fourth occurrence would not need to be forgiven. So Peter was acting generously in suggesting forgiveness for a full seven instances of interpersonal transgression. Perhaps Peter was trying to impress Jesus with his "spiritual progress"?

Question 2. According to Jesus, forgiveness can't be limited by counting. Note that, because the Greek wording is somewhat ambiguous, some versions say: "seventy *times* seven." Other versions translate: "seventy *plus* seven." Either way, the remark means, in effect, that we must be willing to extend unlimited forgiveness or "times without number."

Question 3. Remind your group members that parables do not attempt to answer all questions on a subject or present a complete theological statement. Caution against reading into a parable or making points from its silence. Verse 33 sums up the main point of the parable: "Since God has forgiven us so much, we should be willing to forgive others their relatively petty offences."

To get an idea of the vast difference between the two debts, consider that a denarius was a laborer's daily wage, about nineteen cents. In contrast, the first servant's amount of indebtedness has been calculated at $12 million. The average price paid for a slave was one tenth of a talent. (A talent was a measurement of weight in gold, silver, or iron. See 1 Chron. 29:4, 7 for talent amounts donated to the temple building project.)

Question 4. Participant responses will vary. But keep your group members aware of the immediate biblical context as they consider the question of forgiving from the heart. This passage should not be separated from the procedural steps for conflict resolution laid out in verses 15–20. There is a proper way to forgive *in the church*. It involves both restoration of the offender and (usually) restitution for the victim.

Question 7. Stress the importance of viewing forgiveness as a personal *decision*. In the instant we choose to forgive, we relieve ourselves of a heavy burden, whether the "forgivee" reciprocates or not.

Question 9. People need a clear understanding of the difference between the sin and the sinner. Forgiveness of the actor does not compel us to approve of the actions. We may, however, feel called to help the offender develop new habits or a new life-style in order to avoid future occurrences.

Question 10. People feel the effects of stored emotions in different kinds of bodily tension. Some people get headaches, others get ulcers. Awareness of tension is a first step in confronting inner conflict caused by resentment, bitterness, grief, anger.

Study 4. Are You Prepared for the Inevitable Losses? 2 Corinthians 4:8–9, 16–18

Aim: To recognize and analyze the mid-life task of grieving over losses of youth, health, and vocational dreams.

Question 1. Paul apparently believed that a Christian could be knocked down by life's crises, but never really knocked out.

Point out that the figures of speech he uses in verses 8 and 9 may have been drawn from the language of the athletic contests of that day, especially the Corinthian Games. Or perhaps Paul had in mind either gladiatorial or military combat. "[Paul] pictures himself as a soldier in the most dire straits, yet ever delivered by divine grace. With a few strokes of the pen he describes the successive states of the battle. The warrior is surrounded, hard pressed, driven from the field, struck by the enemies' sword, given over to death, yet marvelously rescued by an unseen Friend" (Charles R. Eerdman, *The Second Epistle of Paul to the Corinthians*, p. 47).

Questions 2 and 3. Paul realistically faced the fact that the "outward man," the physical person, wears out. See his reference to himself in Philemon 9: "Paul, the aged." But Paul did not lose heart because he sensed daily renewal in his inner life with God. No doubt much of this renewal came through his times of prayer and Scripture meditation, and through his fellowship with other believers.

Question 4. "Weight" here was originally the Greek translation of the Hebrew word *kabod*, which means either "weight" or "glory." Glory can be understood as a weightiness when it inspires awe or respect. A "weighty" person has a certain aura—glory—when entering a room. Paul seems to say that the eternal realities will be "heavier" for us someday because they will appear even more real than what we know now.

Some people will be encouraged by such thoughts. Others will regard such pronouncements as mere "pie in the sky" thinking. But Christians should work at seeing the reality of the things promised (see Hebrews 11:1-3, 13-16).

Question 5. Note that Paul is not calling us to disregard the visible world. He simply lifts up the tension between what is already and what is yet to come. God's kingdom—all the eternal things—is yet to be revealed in all its glory. Yet we move closer to it by faith. This renews us and keeps us going.

Study 5. Is the Adolescent in Control, or Are You and Your Spouse?
Luke 2:40-50

Aim: To challenge parents to form a solid front in their parenting approach with teens.

Question 2. Jesus was clearly beginning to assert His own autonomy here. Point out that the gospel writers never intended to give a complete biography of the life of Jesus. They leave out almost the entire adolescence of Jesus (except for this one incident). No doubt there were many other events in which the parents gradually came to see that Jesus had His own integrity as a person—and His own special, divinely-ordained purposes.

Question 3. Be sure everyone recognizes that Jesus had no real reason for being reprimanded. As the sinless Son of God —deity incarnate—Jesus did everything in the right time and in the right way.

Question 4. Mention that the angelic announcements before Jesus' birth may have faded a bit in the minds of His parents. In any case, the understanding of Mary and Joseph remained incomplete. These parents had to come to the gradual realization and acceptance that their son truly was the promised Messiah.

Knowing about, and relating with, the inner life of one's teen is essential. Suicide statistics tell us that a child can have absolutely everything—outwardly, materially—but be in absolute despair over the emotional distance between himself and his parents. Parents must be willing to get deeply involved in an adolescent's emotional life.

Question 7. Stress that one is not doing the child a favor by giving in behind the more resolute partner's back. This is simply a way to bring more confusion into the child's life.

Question 9. Ask your group members to come up with specific examples they have seen in themselves or others of ways parents try to live their lives through their children. What about the Little League dad, for instance, who was never very coordinated. How important is it for his son to be a "winner"?

Question 10. Mention that almost all human progress comes from trial and error. This is how we all learn and grow. This is how science develops theory into fact, for example—through experimentation. And it is how teens try out their adult wings. Sometimes they seem to crash and burn. But we must give our teens the privilege of picking themselves up (with our help) and trying again.

Study 6. Can Your Spouse Fulfill Your Need for Intimacy?
Job 13:20–24

Aim: To identify the warning signs and barriers to intimacy in marriage.

Question 1. Note that Job felt (mistakenly) that he was being rejected by God. His sufferings were understood to be the result of God's displeasure.
Ask your group members to comment on parallels they see between Job's relationship with God and the issues they've studied in this study guide chapter:
—fears of rejection or of being hurt by a spouse;
—false assumptions about a spouse's view of us;
—bargaining or negotiating for needs to be met.

Question 2. Point out that verse 21 can be read in two ways. Job may have asked in his first request that: (1) God would withdraw His hand of *punishment* from Job; or (2) that God would not withdraw His *presence* from Job.

Job's second request is clearer: that God would not be a constant source of fear or anxiety in Job's heart. (Note that a third request comes through in verse 22: "I wish to restore communication with you, God.")

Since God is a personal being, intimacy is also a goal for our relationship with Him. All of Job's requests in this prayer have parallel applications to the marriage relationship. Ask your group members to voice the applications they see.

Question 3. In the spiritual life, people usually have to come to a point of seeing themselves as "lost" before they can "get saved." That is why the Old Testament commandments are so powerful; they clearly reveal our inability to live a perfect life apart from God.

In our relationships, we may also wait for a crisis to reveal our lostness, or desperation, before leveling with ourselves and others. This is unfortunate and can be avoided through practicing the intimacy-deepening methods discussed in this chapter.

Question 6. No marriage is without anger or conflict. The point is, anger and hurt can be buried and covered, or it can be evident in word and deed. Both kinds of conflict—inner and outer—cause marital pain. The latter has a better chance of being resolved because it has been openly "placed on the table."

Question 7. It is so common for the husband, for instance, to treat every bit of pain-sharing by the wife as a "complaint" that needs a verbal "solution." Try to get husbands to admit the tendency to place such sharing into a problem-solving context, immediately making it a cerebral interchange. Usually the wife is looking for an emotional exchange in which comfort and nurture flow. The content of the "problem" typically recedes into the background as the loving relationship meets the real needs.